PROJECT AIR FORCE

T0108563

Supplemental Career Paths for Air Force Pilots

A Warrant Officer Component or an Aviation Technical Track?

Albert A. Robbert, Michael G. Mattock, Beth J. Asch, John S. Crown, James Hosek, Tara L. Terry

Prepared for the United States Air Force
Approved for public release; distribution unlimited

For more information on this publication, visit www.rand.org/t/RR2617

Library of Congress Cataloging-in-Publication Data is available for this publication.
ISBN: 978-1-9774-0090-1

Published by the RAND Corporation, Santa Monica, Calif.
© Copyright 2018 RAND Corporation
RAND® is a registered trademark.

Support RAND
Make a tax-deductible charitable contribution at
www.rand.org/giving/contribute

www.rand.org

Preface

In response to congressional staff interest, the U.S. Air Force Director of Military Force Management Policy asked RAND Project AIR FORCE (PAF) to compare force sustainment and cost considerations for introducing a component within the pilot workforce that is restricted largely to continuous flying duty. We considered two options: a warrant officer component, comparable to the Army aviation warrant officer program, and an aviation technical track for commissioned officers. Neither would replace the current career path but rather would supplement it in ways intended to be retention-enhancing for some segment of the pilot force. We conducted an analysis of the alternatives as a direct-assistance effort, with some supporting analyses performed as part of ongoing work in projects pertaining to aircrew management and pilot retention. Although the concepts examined in this report might be applied in the reserve components, our analysis was limited because of time and resource constraints to the active component. The research reported here was commissioned by the Director of Military Force Management Policy and conducted within the Manpower, Personnel, and Training Program of PAF.

This report should be of value to policymakers interested in exploring potential avenues for managing the Air Force's most critical human capital—its pilot workforce. Pilots are expensive to produce and difficult to retain because of competing economic opportunities. Maintaining an appropriately experienced workforce requires careful calibration of inventory stocks and flows that is easily tipped out of balance. Like with all departures from the currently calibrated system, the potential introduction of alternative human capital approaches should be carefully analyzed.

This report was prepared primarily for a readership familiar with Air Force aircrew management, pilot retention issues, and retention modeling. Deeper background on these issues can be found in various references cited in the report.

RAND Project AIR FORCE

RAND Project AIR FORCE (PAF), a division of the RAND Corporation, is the U.S. Air Force's federally funded research and development center for studies and analyses. PAF provides the Air Force with independent analyses of policy alternatives affecting the development, employment, combat readiness, and support of current and future air, space, and cyber forces. Research is conducted in four programs: Strategy and Doctrine; Force Modernization and Employment; Manpower, Personnel, and Training; and Resource Management. The research reported here was prepared under contract FA7014-16-D-1000.

Additional information about PAF is available on our website: www.rand.org/paf

This report documents work originally shared with the U.S. Air Force on April 19, 2018. The draft report, issued on May 25, 2018, was reviewed by formal peer reviewers and U.S. Air Force subject-matter experts.

Contents

Figures

Tables

Summary

This report documents analyses to help the Air Force Director of Military Force Management Policy respond to a request from congressional staff to consider reimplementation of a warrant officer (WO) program in the Air Force, specifically to fill pilot requirements, or an alternative, an aviation technical track (ATT) for commissioned officers (COs). Either alternative would supplement the traditional pilot career path in a manner intended to enhance force sustainment and thus help to reduce pilot shortages at least cost.

Any shift in management of the Air Force's pilot workforce must be evaluated with due consideration of its centrality to the Air Force's core missions and the difficulty of keeping pilot production, absorption, retention, and overall inventory sustainment in balance. Pilot production and absorption, in particular, are difficult to expand and are often constrained below levels needed to meet requirements. Retention is very sensitive to extrinsic factors, particularly major airline hiring (MAH). With those considerations in mind, we address several key issues in this report:

- Is there room for a WO component or an ATT in the pilot workforce pyramid?
- How would WO or ATT officer retention compare with that of officers in a traditional pilot track?
- How would WO or ATT costs differ from current CO costs?
- Would either the WO or ATT alternative introduce force management risks?

This document provides a quick response to these questions, drawing from RAND Project AIR FORCE capabilities and existing pilot models. In brief, we found that structural considerations would permit either a WO or an ATT component of the officer pilot force, sized at about 1,000 pilots out of a total requirement of a little under 13,000. Most importantly, the WO option would be expected to *reduce* pilot retention, while the ATT would be expected to *increase* it. Cost considerations, although minor, are favorable for both alternatives. Both present risks that merit more consideration than we were able to bring to bear in the analyses yet performed.

A Warrant Officer Component

Force Structure Considerations

We found that there would be headroom in the pilot career force for a WO component but that the amount of headroom would be contingent on CO retention. At current and expected retention levels, a steady-state pilot force produces more field-grade officers (FGOs) (grades O-4 and O-5) than are required.[1] This can be seen currently: The field-grade pilot inventory exceeds requirements, even though there is an overall shortage of pilots. At currently expected retention rates, a field-grade inventory that equals field-grade requirements can be sustained from a company-grade inventory that is less than company-grade requirements. Accordingly, there is room for a WO component to fill a determinable number of company-grade requirements, and perhaps some field-grade requirements. After considering a range of alternative assumptions regarding traditional-track officer retention and the acceptability of placing WOs in what are currently field-grade positions, we concluded that a component of about 1,000 WOs would be prudent.

Retention

We estimate that WO retention rates would be lower than those of COs in most of the cases we examined. Using RAND's Dynamic Retention Model, we obtained results for multiple aviation communities, two Aviation Bonus (AvB) levels ($25,000 and $35,000 per year), and two MAH levels (1,700 and 3,200 per year). COs tend to have better retention than WOs in these analyses due to a smaller difference between military compensation and the civilian opportunity wage for COs than for WOs.

Costs

We estimate that a WO component would be less costly than the corresponding number of COs whom the WOs would displace. The net cost includes two offsetting considerations. A WO component would incur lower *personnel* costs, including basic pay and allowances and special and incentive pays—notably, Aviation Incentive Pay (AvIP) and AvB—and the retirement accrual charge. However, because of lower retention expectations, higher training pipeline throughput would be required, at a variable *training* cost of $1 million to $6.7 million for undergraduate and graduate (system-specific) training, depending on the aircraft system.[2] At the retention levels we anticipate, personnel cost savings would slightly exceed training cost increases, yielding potential net savings of $4 million to $30 million (roughly 1 percent of total pilot personnel and training costs), depending on the retention environment and on the distribution of WOs across various aircrew communities.

Risks

WO retention would be more sensitive than CO retention to MAH levels, requiring greater flexibility in AvB management. Moreover, if a WO component were sized to complement a

---

[1] Per Air Force aircrew management convention, O-6s are not counted as part of the pilot workforce.

[2] An alternative approach to sustaining force size by increasing accessions would be to offer higher AvB to WOs to increase retention, thereby avoiding the higher training costs. We did not evaluate this alternative, although it might be less costly than the estimates for WOs that we provide.

company-grade CO inventory that just sustained field-grade requirements, both field-grade and total pilot shortages would occur if CO retention dipped below the planned level. Finally, the increased pilot production needed with a WO component might exceed feasible production or absorption capacities.

An Aviation Technical Track

As an alternative to reintroduction of WOs in the Air Force, we examined a close alternative—implementation of an ATT for COs. To evaluate this alternative, we first had to define its essential characteristics. The concept generally includes providing a limited number of COs a career path that is focused exclusively, or nearly so, on jobs that require continuous flying duties. It would target officers who miss key developmental opportunities or who would prefer to forgo such opportunities.

To provide a retention-enhancing career path, the track should provide

- a defined duty set
- greater assignment stability
- predictable, reasonably attractive promotion outcomes
- a clear path to retirement by removing risks of involuntary separation.

Force Structure Considerations

Almost every nonflying position requiring a pilot is at the field-grade level. Thus, there is no significant benefit in entering officers into an ATT prior to their selection for promotion to O-4. We recommend entry into the ATT at the grades of O-4 and O-5 at points after selection for promotion to either of those grades but prior to in-the-promotion-zone (IPZ) consideration to the next-higher grade. If the ATT becomes attractive enough to draw more interested applicants than its targeted size will accommodate, a competitive selection process will be needed. Off-ramps back to the line of the Air Force (LAF) would be permitted, up to the point at which an ATT officer's LAF cohort is considered IPZ for the next grade.

Because officers in the ATT would bypass key developmental experiences, their promotion expectations should be diminished relative to those of officers in a traditional track but sufficient to motivate entry into the ATT. This outcome can be managed by placing officers in the ATT in their own competitive category, separate from the LAF competitive category in which most Air Force officers are considered for promotion. Table S.1 indicates our recommended promotion parameters.

Table S.1. Current Line of the Air Force and Recommended Aviation Technical-Track Promotion Parameters

Grade	Competitive Category	Opportunity, as a Percentage	IPZ Timing (Pin-On), in CYOSs	IPZ Timing (Board Date), in CYOSs	Below-the-Promotion-Zone Consideration
O-5	Current LAF	~85	~15	14	Yes
	Recommended ATT	~50	~18	17	No
O-6	Current LAF	~50	~21	20	Yes
	Recommended ATT	~25	~24	23	No

NOTE: CYOS = commissioned year of service.

Assignment policies would clearly define the sets of jobs to which ATT officers would be assignable, although policies could flexibly allow ATT officers to volunteer for nonflying positions. Four years minimum time on station would be guaranteed except under defined conditions. Assignment policies for grounded pilots would also be established.

Rather than identifying specific manpower authorizations as ATT billets, ATT and traditional-track officers would be assigned flexibly against a common subset of flying requirements. Distribution of grade ceilings to the ATT competitive category would be based on desired promotion outcomes rather than manpower grade requirements.

The ATT must be sized so that potential adverse impacts on traditional-track officers are minimized—chiefly, the proportion of time spent in nonflying assignments. Too high a proportion could reduce retention of those remaining in the traditional track. We estimate that 28 percent of field-grade pilots are currently serving in nonflying positions. If expected retention rates prevail over a long enough period, this proportion will rise to an estimated 32 percent. Table S.2 indicates how large the ATT could grow as a function of limits on this proportion. We recommend a limit of 40 percent, yielding a recommended ATT size of about 1,000 officers.

Table S.2. Aviation Technical-Track Size as a Function of Limits on Nonflying Assignments for Traditional-Track Field-Grade Officers

FGOs	Percentage of Traditional-Track FGOs in Nonflying Positions			
	35	40	45	50
Traditional track in flying positions	3,005	2,427	1,978	1,618
Traditional track in nonflying positions	1,618	1,618	1,618	1,618
Total traditional track	4,623	4,045	3,596	3,236
ATT	409	987	1,437	1,796
Total	5,032	5,032	5,032	5,032

SOURCE: Position requirements: Air Force Total Force Aircrew Management Office.
NOTE: Because of rounding, some totals do not sum precisely.

Retention

We reason that the ATT would be appealing to officers with weaker career paths who see the ATT as a way to improve their promotion prospects and to officers with stronger career paths who see it as more satisfying than the traditional track and are willing to accept lower promotion prospects in order to obtain it. Available aircrew survey data strongly support these suppositions. However, as discussed above, potential negative retention impacts on traditional-track officers must be minimized by limiting the size of the ATT.

Costs

With increased retention, the year-of-service distribution in grades O-4 and O-5 would be expected to increase slightly as a result of longer tenures of ATT officers in those grades, slightly increasing average rates of pay. However, better retention would also reduce pilot production requirements, lowering training costs. We estimate that the training cost reductions would be greater than the personnel cost increases, yielding a net cost reduction.

Risks

Risks arise from uncertainties that could affect the rate of retention of officers in the traditional track. These include the impact of an increased proportion of nonflying assignments, adverse promotion outcomes, reduced availability of aviation service needed to maximize pilots' AvIP eligibility, and reduced experience in *operational* squadrons prior to assignment as squadron commanders. Except for the proportion of nonflying assignments, we believe that these risks are minimal, but they merit further investigation prior to implementation of an ATT.

Conclusions

Table S.3 summarizes the findings of this quick-response study. Because the fundamental objective of either supplemental path is to enhance retention, particularly when demand for commercial pilots is high, the ATT is clearly favored. Both alternatives would yield modest cost savings, and both would present risks yet to be fully evaluated. Not least significant is that a WO program would require development and management of new processes and policies across the personnel life cycle—recruiting, accessions, compensation, retention, utilization, promotion, and transition. An ATT would require much less sweeping adjustments, most of which would be managed through the creation of a new competitive category.

Table S.3. Comparison of Key Factors

Factor	WO Component	ATT
Retention	−	+
Production and absorption requirements	+	−
Personnel costs	−	+
Training costs	+	−
Net costs	−	−
Administrative requirements	+ Need to manage the life cycle of a new personnel category	− Need to establish a new competitive category
Risks	Retention is more sensitive to MAH; possible field-grade and total pilot shortages if retention is less than planned	Possible retention impacts on traditional-track officers (more nonflying assignments, adverse promotion outcomes, missing third AvIP gates, less operational experience)

Abbreviations

ADSC	active-duty service commitment
AF/A3TF	Air Force Total Force Aircrew Management office
APZ	above the promotion zone
ATT	aviation technical track
AvB	Aviation Bonus
AvIP	Aviation Incentive Pay
C2ISR	command, control, intelligence, surveillance, and reconnaissance
CGO	company-grade officer
CO	commissioned officer
CYOS	commissioned year of service
DoD	U.S. Department of Defense
DRM	Dynamic Retention Model
FGO	field-grade officer
FY	fiscal year
IPZ	in the promotion zone
LAF	line of the Air Force
MAH	major airline hiring
NCP	normal cost percentage
PAF	RAND Project AIR FORCE
RMC	regular military compensation
TARS	total active rated service
WO	warrant officer
YOS	year of service

Acknowledgments

The objectives pursued in this report and its underlying analyses were defined by Maj Gen Robert D. LaBrutta, Air Force Director of Military Force Management Policy, and our analyses were informed by discussions with him and others from his office—notably, Col William D. Fischer and Emi Izawa. Michael A. Torino of the Air Force Total Force Aircrew Management Office provided the pilot requirement data that underlie much of the analyses. RAND colleagues Peter Schirmer, Michael Boito, and David Schulker provided critical reviews, and the report benefited from careful editing by Lisa Bernard. Any remaining errors are, of course, our own.

Chapter One. Introduction

This report provides analysis to help the U.S. Air Force Director of Military Force Management Policy respond to a request from congressional staff to consider reimplementation of a warrant officer (WO) program in the Air Force, specifically to fill pilot requirements, or an alternative, an aviation technical track (ATT) for commissioned officers (COs). Either alternative would supplement the traditional pilot career path, engaging those who follow it in continuous flying activity, thus avoiding both nonflying assignments that require pilot qualifications and nonaviation career-broadening assignment or educational opportunities. Both initiatives are intended to enhance the retention of pilots who might prefer a so-called fly-only track, thereby helping the Air Force to address its persistent pilot shortage.

The Air Force has had WOs in the past. When the Air Force separated from the Army in 1947, it inherited an inventory of 1,230 WOs and continued to accession new WOs, reaching a peak inventory of 4,541 in 1957 and 1958 (Jones, 2008). However, when the E-8 and E-9 enlisted grades (or *supergrades*, as they were called at the time) were established in 1958, the Air Force phased out its WO program because the duties envisioned for these senior enlisted grades were similar to those performed by WOs. The last Air Force WO retired in 1980.

Does it make sense for the Air Force to once again have WOs—specifically, to have WO pilots? Is the ATT a better alternative? This document provides a quick response to these questions, drawing from RAND Project AIR FORCE (PAF) capabilities and existing pilot models. We address several key issues:

- Is there room for a WO component or an ATT in the pilot career force pyramid?
- How would WO or ATT retention compare with that of officers in a traditional pilot track?
- How would WO or ATT costs differ from current CO costs?
- Would either the WO or ATT option introduce force management risks?

As this report documents, we found that structural considerations would permit either a WO or an ATT component of the officer pilot force, sized at about 1,000 pilots out of a total requirement of a little under 13,000. Most importantly for the primary objective of introducing either component to the pilot workforce, the WO option would be expected to *reduce* pilot retention, while the ATT would be expected to *increase* it. Cost considerations, although minor, are favorable for both alternatives. Both alternatives present risks that merit more consideration than we were able to bring to bear in the analyses yet performed.

A Uniquely Critical Workforce

Any shift in management of the Air Force's pilot workforce must be evaluated with due consideration of its centrality to the Air Force's core missions and its tightly constrained structural dynamics.

Air Force Pilot Roles

Pilots perform critical operational tasks in the Air Force's largest, longest-standing core functions. They also form the largest and generally the most senior segment of the Air Force's internal military leadership and its contribution to joint warfighting leadership.

The Air Force pilot force can be disaggregated into several categories. As of September 2017, COs rated for operation of manned aircraft numbered 12,002 in the active component and 6,485 in reserve components. Additionally, 1,562 COs (as of October 2017) and 15 enlisted personnel (as of January 2018) are part of a growing force rated for operation of remotely piloted aircraft. Smaller numbers of civilian pilots are employed in test, development, and training roles, and a growing number of contractors provide pilots in adversary air roles that support continuation training of military pilots. In this analysis, we focused on active-component COs rated as pilots of manned aircraft because they differ significantly from those in other categories in terms of numbers, training costs, service commitments, and retention characteristics.

Aircrew Management Dynamics

A key pilot inventory management challenge for the Air Force is to fill its cockpit and noncockpit pilot requirements through production of new pilots at rates that do not exceed the absorption capacity of its operational units (Taylor, Moore, and Roll, 2000; Taylor, Bigelow, Moore, et al., 2002; Taylor, Bigelow, and Ausink, 2009; Robbert, Rosello, et al., 2015).[1] Absorption capacity—most acute in fighter units—is related to practical limits on the proportion of inexperienced pilots in an operational unit. These limits are due in part to the scarcity of flying-hours needed to season inexperienced pilots so that they can advance from copilot to pilot or wingman to flight lead and on to more-advanced roles (Bigelow, Taylor, et al., 2003).[2]

Absorption capacity limits the long-run size of total pilot inventory. In a steady state, the maximum size of a healthy active-duty inventory equals annual absorption capacity multiplied by the expected years of total active rated service (TARS). TARS, in turn, is a function of pilot

---

[1] In this context, *production* refers to the output of undergraduate and graduate pilot training pipelines and *absorption* refers to the process and the capacity for introducing pipeline graduates into their first operational units.

[2] In fighter units, experience and analysis indicate that inexperienced pilots should be no more than 45 percent of the total pilot strength of a squadron. Upgrade to an experienced level takes close to three years at prevailing sortie rates. Thus, annual absorption capacity is roughly one-third of 45 percent, or 15 percent, of a squadron's authorized pilot strength. If absorption capacity is exceeded, scarce sortie capacity results in extending the time needed for inexperienced pilots to reach an experienced level, an unfavorable distribution of flying-hours between experienced and inexperienced pilots, and overall reduced readiness of the unit.

active-duty service commitments (ADSCs) and retention. Even with ten-year ADSCs following completion of pilot training, the Air Force struggles to retain enough pilots to meet its requirements for approximately 11,200 cockpit and 1,700 noncockpit pilots.[3] The proven strategy for doing so at least cost is to maximize absorption capacity while funding sufficient pipeline training capacity, flying-hours, and retention incentives to keep the force in balance (Bigelow and Robbert, 2011).

Although these dynamics can be seen in their net effect across the total pilot force, they play out differently in various communities in the pilot force. Of these categories (fighter; bomber; mobility; command, control, intelligence, surveillance, and reconnaissance [C2ISR]; combat search and rescue; trainer; special operations; and unmanned), the fighter community is the most tightly constrained because of its limited absorption capacity.

An additional consideration is the need to meet senior leadership requirements that, in the Air Force, are filled disproportionately by pilots.[4] This requires sufficient company-grade officers (CGOs) to sustain field-grade requirements and sufficient field-grade officers (FGOs) with the right experience to provide a strong bench from which to choose general officers. It requires time out of the cockpit in positions that develop competencies in joint warfighting and various nonflying functions.

Basis for This Report

Development of this report tapped into PAF's extensive experience in providing analytic support for the Air Force's management of its aircrew resources. In other aspects of this work, PAF routinely provides multiyear projections of aircrew inventories. PAF also periodically provides analyses of interacting pilot production, absorption, and retention interactions and, using its Dynamic Retention Model (DRM), of the effects of alternative pilot-specific compensation policies.

Organization of This Report

Chapter Two provides analysis of force sustainment considerations, retention, cost, and risk pertinent to the introduction of WO pilots. Chapter Three examines similar considerations for an ATT for COs. Chapter Four provides our overall conclusions.

---

[3] Per Air Force aircrew management convention, these numbers are for positions in the grades of O-1 through O-5. Positions and pilots in the grade of O-6 are managed separately from the dynamics described in this paragraph.

[4] Organizations generally find that their effectiveness is enhanced by drawing senior leadership from the occupations or professions that are most closely identified with their core missions. For an extended discussion, see Mosher (1982).

Chapter Two. A Warrant Officer Component

Force Structure Considerations

If introduced into the Air Force as pilots, WOs would most likely take roles currently performed by company-grade COs. All WOs are junior to all COs, so it would be inappropriate to place WOs in field-grade positions that require the supervision of COs. Moreover, in a comprehensive review of Army, Navy, and Marine Corps WO programs, Fernandez (2002) saw having WOs as a higher-retention alternative to enlisted service for filling highly technical positions rather than as an alternative to commissioned service. It is possible that WOs would fill some field-grade staff positions requiring technical depth but no supervision of officer subordinates, but these positions would be very limited. In our analysis, we generally considered WOs to fill company-grade positions, with an excursion to examine a small proportion (5 percent) filling field-grade positions.

In 2018, the Air Force Total Force Aircrew Management office (AF/A3TF) estimated 12,930 pilot requirements in grades O-1 through O-5.[1] This figure is an estimate because some portion of officer requirements are either not linked to a specific Air Force specialty code (the students, transients, and patients account) or are cross-occupational positions that can be filled by either pilots or nonpilots (referred to as *institutional requirements*). The number of requirements for pilots in student, transient, or patient status or filling institutional requirements must be estimated from past representation of pilots in those categories. The grade distribution of these requirements and the current corresponding inventory are shown in Table 2.1.

---

[1] In this section of the report, *field grade* refers to grades O-4 and O-5 and *total officers* refers to grades O-1 through O-5. In Air Force aircrew management processes, O-6s are considered to be outside of the aircrew force. We follow that convention in most but not all parts of this document.

Table 2.1. Fiscal Year 2018 Pilot Requirements and Inventory

Grade	Requirements	Inventory
O-5	1,893	2,386
O-4	2,716	3,212
O-3	4,284	5,023
O-1 and O-2	4,037	1,381
Field grade	4,609	5,598
Company grade	8,321	6,404
Total (the sum of O-1–O-5 rows or field plus company grades)	12,930	12,002
Field grade as a percentage of the total	36%	47%

SOURCES: Requirements: Manpower Programming and Execution System and AF/A3TF estimates; inventory: Air Force personnel data file as of September 2017.

Although Table 2.1 shows that the Air Force is currently contending with an overall shortage of about 900 pilots, it also shows surpluses at the field-grade level. Against the field-grade requirement of 4,609, there were 5,598 field-grade pilots in the inventory as of September 2017. The field-grade surplus occurs because the grade distribution of pilot requirements is lean relative to the overall line officer grade distribution. Field-grade pilot requirements are 36 percent of total pilot requirements (4,609 divided by 12,930), while, for all line officer requirements, both field-grade manpower authorizations and the line competitive category's allocated share of statutory field-grade ceilings (for promotion and grade management purposes) are 40 percent of the total. Because pilots are generally promoted at or above averages for all line officers, they tend to build up an inventory that is at least 40 percent field grade while requirements are 36 percent field grade. The effect is magnified by pilot retention that is higher than overall line officer retention because of the ten-year ADSC for pilots and extensive use of retention bonuses for pilots. The current inventory, as shown in Table 2.1, formed by higher past retention and pilot production patterns, is 47 percent field grade.

To determine the headroom available for WOs, we constructed steady-state profiles for COs that match the current field-grade requirement while allowing the company-grade base to assume whatever size and shape is needed to sustain the field-grade requirement. If the company-grade sustaining base is less than the company-grade requirement, the difference can be considered headroom that could be filled by WOs. Figure 2.1 shows this construct for two different retention assumptions. The "higher retention" bars show the expected distribution using fiscal year (FY) 2017 retention experience adjusted for the expected impacts of increased major airline hiring (MAH). The "lower retention" bars show the distribution if retention were to decline to levels observed between FY 1996 and 2016 (again, adjusted for anticipated MAH).[2] Officers are

---

[2] In FY 2017, MAH had ramped up from previous periods, but the Aviation Bonus (AvB) rate had been increased from $25,000 to $35,000 per year and made available for shorter commitment periods; Aviation Incentive

currently promoted to O-4 at very near ten years of service (YOSs) at a very high (virtually 100-percent) rate. Thus, the sum of inventory in commissioned YOSs (CYOSs) 10 through 28 is a reasonable approximation of the expected field-grade inventory. In both cases, the field-grade inventory is sized to be exactly 4,609 (the field-grade requirement from Table 2.1). The company-grade base required to sustain it is 7,234 in the higher-retention case. When added to the field-grade requirement, the total is 11,843, of which 39 percent is field grade. In the lower-retention case, the company-grade base is 8,285, resulting in a total of 12,894, of which 36 percent is field grade.

Figure 2.1. Expected Steady-State Pilot Inventories: Company-Grade Inventories Sized to Sustain Field-Grade Requirements

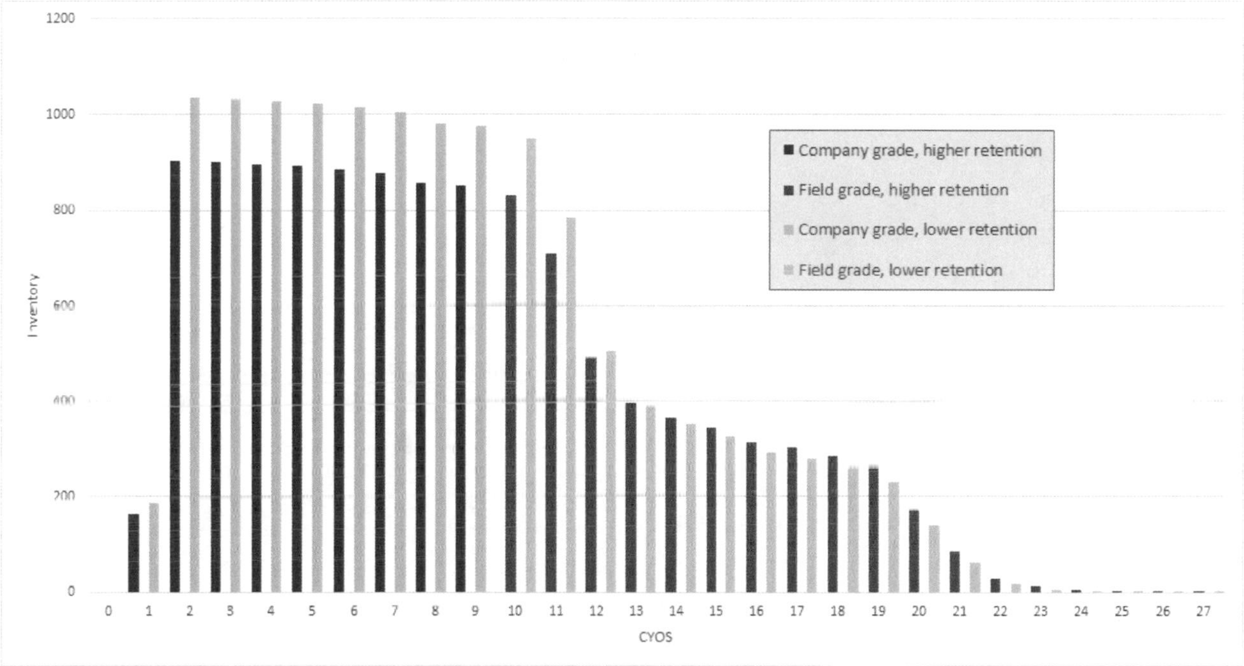

SOURCES: Field-grade requirements: AF/A3TF.
NOTE: We derived these profiles from aircrew management methodologies, which regard O-6s as being out of the pilot force; accordingly, promotion to O-6 is treated as a loss. Thus, expected field-grade inventories shown in this figure include only O-4s and O-5s.

Table 2.2 compares the headroom available for WO pilots under both of the retention assumptions shown in Figure 2.1 and under two different assumptions regarding WO utilization. In one case, WOs are assumed to fill only company-grade requirements; alternatively, they are assumed to also fill 5 percent of field-grade requirements. In the case most favorable to

Pay (AvIP) rates were also increased. Although the positive impact of the AvB and AvIP changes appears to have been greater than the negative impact of increased airline hiring, further increases in airline hiring could overwhelm compensation effects, possibly resulting in reversion to something like the lower retention levels depicted in Figure 2.1.

introducing WOs into the pilot inventory, we estimate that headroom would be available for 1,679 WOs, leaving sufficient company-grade CO strength to sustain field-grade requirements. In the least favorable case, we see headroom for only 36 WOs.

Table 2.2. Estimated Warrant Officer Headroom

Fill	Higher-Retention Inventories		Lower-Retention Inventories	
	WOs Fill Only Company-Grade Requirements	WOs Also Fill 5% of Field-Grade Requirements	WOs Fill Only Company-Grade Requirements	WOs Also Fill 5% of Field-Grade Requirements
Company-grade requirements				
Filled by COs	7,234	6,872	8,285	7,870
Filled by WOs	1,087	1,449	36	451
Total	8,321	8,321	8,321	8,321
Field-grade requirements				
Filled by COs	4,609	4,379	4,609	4,379
Filled by WOs		230		230
Total	4,609	4,609	4,609	4,609
Total requirements				
Filled by COs	11,843	11,251	12,894	12,249
Filled by WOs	1,087	1,679	36	681
Total	12,930	12,930	12,930	12,930

The most likely of these cases is the higher-retention case in which WOs fill only company-grade requirements. This would result in a planned WO inventory of 1,087. A WO inventory of this size would be dwarfed by the overall size of the officer and enlisted inventories of the Air Force. Introducing the additional management burdens of a new category of personnel (separate policies, procedures, and programs for accessions, promotions, assignments, and other personnel management functions) would be worthwhile only if having that new category provided a significant advantage in sustaining the pilot force or if that burden were offset by substantial cost savings or other force management considerations. Additionally, if the very real possibility of lower pilot retention prevailed, the reduced company-grade base would no longer be adequate to support field-grade requirements. In the rest of this chapter, we explore those considerations.

Retention

As shown in Figure 2.2, Army aviation WO retention patterns are dissimilar to the patterns exhibited by two representative Air Force pilot communities. An Army WO has a shorter ADSC after completing flying training (six years versus ten years), less generous AvB retention incentives, and no prospect of being hired as a major airline pilot. Accordingly, we could not adapt Army aviation WO retention data for use in our analysis. We had to find an alternative way to estimate the retention behavior of WO pilots in the Air Force.

Figure 2.2. Air Force Pilot Versus Army Aviation Warrant Officer Retention Profiles

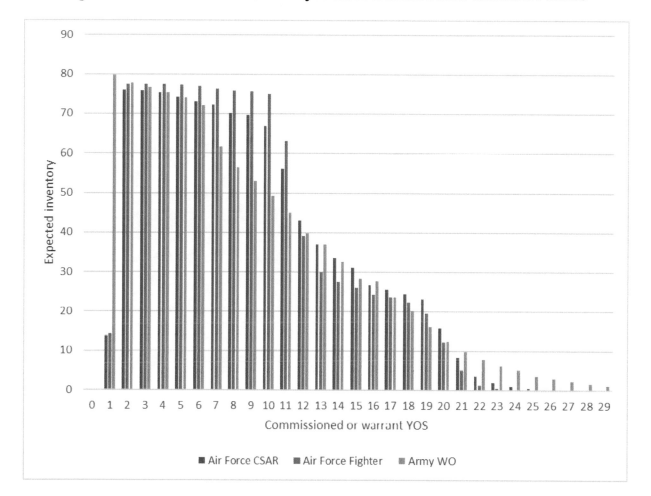

SOURCES: Army Personnel Command data; Air Force Personnel Center data transformed by RAND modeling.
NOTE: *n* = 1,000. CSAR = combat search and rescue. These Air Force profiles, like those shown in Figure 2.1, were derived from aircrew management methodologies, which regard O-6s as being out of the pilot force; accordingly, promotion to O-6 is treated as a loss.

For our analysis, we generated retention expectations for WOs using RAND's DRM. The DRM has been described in earlier documents, including one pertaining to Air Force pilots (Mattock et al., 2016). Using parameters developed from longitudinal retention data, alternative military and civilian earnings, MAH levels, and other pertinent data, the model can be used to project pilot retention under a variety of assumed conditions.

Coefficients used in the model have been estimated for pilots who are COs but not for pilots who are WOs. For this analysis, we assumed that the behavior of WO pilots would differ from that of COs only because of differences in their military compensation (lower for WOs) and in the compensation they would receive as nonpilots after separation from the military (also lower

9

for WOs).[3] Results are specific to various aviator communities (communities examined in this analysis were fighter, mobility, trainer, C2ISR, and bomber) because estimated propensities to separate and to take airline pilot jobs after separation vary widely among these communities.

Figure 2.3 illustrates the expected inventory profiles of CO and WO mobility pilots under various retention assumptions. These results were obtained from the DRM with AvB capped at either $25,000 or $35,000 per year and with an assumption that MAH would total 3,200 pilots per year. Total inventory depicted in each profile is 1,000, which approximates the targeted number of WOs displacing COs in the first case listed in Table 2.2 (high retention; WOs fill only field-grade requirements). As expected, the higher AvB cap yields better retention for both COs and WOs. COs have better retention than WOs because of a smaller difference between military compensation and the civilian opportunity wage for COs than for WOs when MAH is at 3,200 per year.

---

[3] The DRM estimates the proportion of Air Force pilots who separate to fly for commercial airlines as a function of MAH. The model parameter estimates are based on empirical data on the active retention and reserve-component participation career histories of officer pilots who were accessioned between 1990 and 2000 and then followed through 2012. When we estimated for COs, we assumed that the same proportion of separating WOs would be employed as airline pilots; we also assumed that nonpilot employment compensation for separated WOs would be less than that of COs because of their lower educational attainment. The civilian expected-wage trajectory used in the model is a weighted average of pilot and nonpilot compensation.

Figure 2.3. Expected Inventory Profiles for Commissioned and Warrant Officer Mobility Pilots

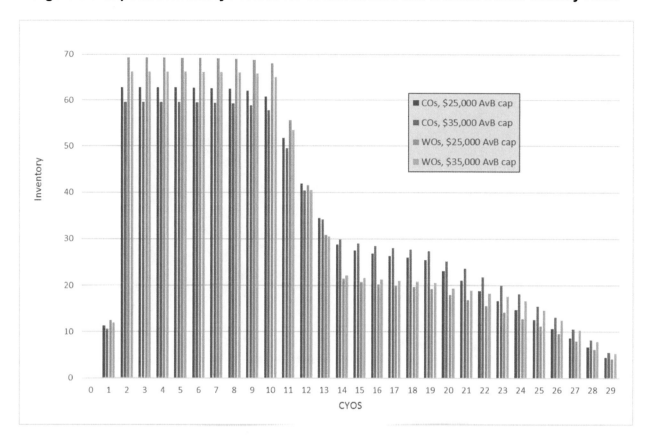

SOURCE: DRM using data from myriad sources.
NOTE: n = 1,000. Because the DRM does not have a grade dimension, this figure differs from Figures 2.1 and 2.2 in that O-6s are not excluded from the inventories. The profiles in Figure 2.1 and parts of Figure 2.2 are similar to those shown here but differ in some respects because of varying underlying methodologies. We derived Figures 2.1 and 2.2 from aircrew management methodologies, which regard O-6s as being out of the pilot force; accordingly, there, promotion to O-6 is treated as a loss. We derived this figure from the DRM, using more-complex retention rate estimations and retaining O-6s as part of the force.
In practice, WO pilots would likely be spread more broadly across aircrew communities rather than concentrated in only one. For simplicity and clarity here, we use mobility pilot dynamics as broadly representative of the entire pilot force.

At either AvB level, the new pilot production requirement for the WO cases is six to seven per year higher than the CO cases. Although these numbers seem small, the long-run impact if pilot production and absorption capacities cannot be scaled up to accommodate them is an inventory shortage about 13 times the production shortfall, or about 80 to 90 pilots. This shortage could be addressed by offering higher levels of AvB to WOs, although we do not consider that case here.

Costs

Cost considerations for pilot careers can be broken down into two major components: *personnel* costs and *training* costs. Personnel costs include basic pay and allowances and special and incentive pays, notably AvIP and AvB, and the retirement accrual charge.

Personnel Costs

More precisely, personnel costs are calculated based on regular military compensation (RMC), which is the sum of basic pay, basic allowance for subsistence, basic allowance for housing, and the federal income tax advantage (due to allowances being nontaxable). The retirement accrual charge is the normal cost percentage (NCP) set by the U.S. Department of Defense (DoD) Office of the Actuary multiplied by the amount of basic pay. The NCP payable by the Air Force for full-time personnel is 28.4 percent in FY 2018 (DoD, 2017, p. 53). Table 2.3 shows the difference in RMC and the retirement accrual charge at comparable career points for various CO and WO grades. In the DRM, we also account for AvIP and AvB.

Table 2.3. Comparison of Commissioned and Warrant Officer Pay: Selected Pay Components, Fiscal Year 2018 Annual Rates

	COs				WOs				
YOS	Grade	RMC	NCP	Total	Grade	RMC	NCP	Total	Difference
1	O-1	61,892	10,592	72,484	W-1	63,255	10,350	73,605	−1,121
3	O-2	83,976	16,004	99,980	W-2	76,886	13,254	90,140	9,840
9	O-3	104,690	20,731	125,421	W-3	88,708	16,410	105,118	20,303
15	O-4	130,256	26,061	156,317	W-4	106,890	21,038	127,928	28,389
22	O-5	154,498	31,626	186,124	W-5	131,242	27,267	158,509	27,615

SOURCES: RMC and base pay used in NCP calculations obtained from Office of the Under Secretary of Defense for Personnel and Readiness (2018), using weighted force distributions by family size for housing allowances.

Although the comparison of comparable career points in Table 2.3 is useful, note that the expected distributions of COs and WOs depicted in Figure 2.3 make these comparisons somewhat less relevant. Because of their lower expected retention rates, WOs would be more heavily represented at the lower end of the pay table and less heavily represented at the high end. This retention pattern contributes to even lower personnel costs than those implied by Table 2.3 for a WO force comparable in size to a CO force.

Training Costs

A key component of the cost of a military pilot force is the set of expenses associated with undergraduate and graduate training pipelines. Table 2.4 provides our estimates of variable and total pipeline training costs for various systems. The methodology for compiling these costs involved retrieving data from the Air Force Total Ownership Cost system on aircraft operating and support costs, determining fixed and variable costs, and calculating the cost per flying-hour at each stage of training. Costs per flying-hour were multiplied by flying-hours from each system's training syllabus to determine the full training cost.

Table 2.4. Variable and Total Costs for Pilot Training Pipelines, in Millions of Fiscal Year 2018 Dollars

System	Variable Cost	Total Cost
A-10	3.9	6.0
F-16	3.7	5.6
F-22	6.7	10.9
C-17	1.0	1.1
C-130J	1.6	2.5
KC-135	1.1	1.2
B-1	4.8	7.3
B-2	6.0	9.9
B-52	6.0	9.7
RC-135	3.8	5.4

SOURCES: Data from the Air Force Total Ownership Cost system and flying-hours from various training syllabi.

Total Per Capita Costs

Training costs can be calculated for the production required to support an inventory profile, added to the personnel costs required for the profile, and divided by the total size of the profile to determine the per capita cost of meeting requirements. Figures 2.4 through 2.6 show steady-state per capita costs for CO and WO inventories in five representative systems across a range of AvB caps with MAH at 3,200 pilots per year.

Figure 2.4. Per Capita Costs for Mobility Systems Under Varying Aviation Bonus Caps

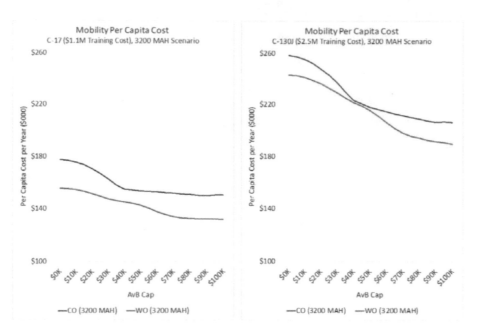

SOURCE: DRM output.

Figure 2.5. Per Capita Costs for Fighter Systems Under Varying Aviation Bonus Caps

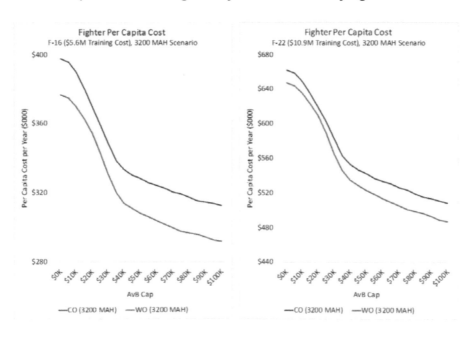

SOURCE: DRM output.

Figure 2.6. Per Capita Costs for a Command, Control, Intelligence, Surveillance, and Reconnaissance System Under Varying Aviation Bonus Caps

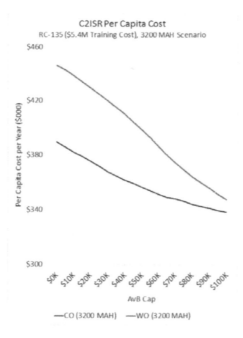

SOURCE: DRM output.

Tables 2.5 through 2.8 show per capita cost differences at various annual MAH levels and AvB cap levels.

Table 2.5. Expected Per Capita Cost Differences with a $25,000 Aviation Bonus Cap and Major Airline Hiring at 3,200 Per Year

System	CO Per Capita Annual Cost, in Dollars	Cost Difference (CO Cost Minus WO Cost), in Dollars	Cost Difference as Percentage of CO Per Capita Cost
C-17	167,000	18,000	10.5
C-130J	243,000	10,000	4.2
F-16	359,000	16,000	4.6
F-22	602,000	13,000	2.2
RC-135	372,000	−53,000	−14.2

SOURCE: DRM output.
NOTE: Because of rounding, some percentages do not appear precisely correct.

15

Table 2.6. Expected Per Capita Cost Differences with a $35,000 Aviation Bonus Cap and Major Airline Hiring at 3,200 Per Year

System	CO Per Capita Annual Cost, in Dollars	Cost Difference (CO Cost Minus WO Cost), in Dollars	Cost Difference as Percentage of CO Per Capita Cost
C-17	158,000	12,000	7.6
C-130J	230,000	4,000	1.7
F-16	339,000	18,000	5.3
F-22	563,000	17,000	3.0
RC-135	365,000	−50,000	−13.6

SOURCE: DRM output.
NOTE: Because of rounding, some percentages do not appear precisely correct.

Table 2.7. Expected Per Capita Cost Differences with a $25,000 Aviation Bonus Cap and Major Airline Hiring at 1,700 Per Year

System	CO Per Capita Annual Cost, in Dollars	Cost Difference (CO Cost Minus WO Cost), in Dollars	Cost Difference as Percentage of CO Per Capita Cost
C-17	158,000	23,000	14.7
C-130J	226,000	25,000	11.1
F-16	351,000	28,000	7.9
F-22	586,000	35,000	6.0
RC-135	344,000	16,000	4.7

SOURCE: DRM output.
NOTE: Because of rounding, some percentages do not appear precisely correct.

Table 2.8. Expected Per Capita Cost Differences with a $35,000 Aviation Bonus Cap and Major Airline Hiring at 1,700 Per Year

System	CO Per Capita Annual Cost, in Dollars	Cost Difference (CO Cost Minus WO Cost), in Dollars	Cost Difference as Percentage of CO Per Capita Cost
C-17	151,000	21,000	13.8
C-130J	215,000	24,000	11.0
F-16	333,000	26,000	7.7
F-22	552,000	31,000	5.6
RC-135	340,000	17,000	5.0

SOURCE: DRM output.
NOTE: Because of rounding, some percentages do not appear precisely correct.

Figure 2.6 reveals the possibility that, in some circumstances, the WO force could be more expensive than the CO force. This occurs because C2ISR pilots have a much greater likelihood than mobility or fighter pilots to separate and take airline pilot jobs, which makes the expected weighted average of airline and nonairline compensation exceptionally high for WOs who would have been C2ISR pilots. This inversion results in a negative entry for the C2ISR system (RC-135) at high MAH levels.

With an additional assumption, the per capita cost differences shown in Tables 2.5 through 2.8 can be extended to determine how an appropriately sized WO component in the pilot force would affect the overall cost of that force. An inventory of 1,000 WOs would constitute 7.7 percent of the 12,930 pilots currently required by the Air Force. Assuming that WO pilots would be proportionately distributed to all aircraft systems, the per capita percentage cost differences shown in these tables can be transformed to reflect total pilot force cost changes. As an example, if the 7.6-percent change in C-17 per capita pilot costs shown in Table 2.6 affects 7.7 percent of the C-17 pilot force, the overall impact on the cost of the C-17 pilot force would be 0.6 percent. Savings for the other three systems with potential cost savings would range from 0.1 to 1.1 percent, while the RC-135 force cost would increase by 1.0 percent in one scenario.

The preceding cost comparisons assume that pipeline training costs for COs and WOs would be identical except for minor differences in the pay of the trainees. But that assumption might not hold. With less education and life experience, WOs' attrition rates from pilot training could be higher or WOs might require additional preparatory training. We thus calculated the allowable increases and percentage changes in WO training costs such that WO and CO per capita costs would be the same. The results are in Table 2.9.

Table 2.9. Expected Cost Increase Margins and Percentage Changes Available for Additional Warrant Officer Training

System	Available Cost Increase Margin, in Dollars	Percentage Change
C-17	400,000	8
C-130J	400,000	4
F-16	200,000	14
F-22	100,000	3
RC-135	−800,000	−15

SOURCE: DRM output.
NOTE: The scenario assumes a $35,000 AvB cap and MAH at 3,200 pilots per year.

Risks

Our analysis revealed that WO retention would be more sensitive than CO retention to MAH levels, requiring greater flexibility in AvB management in order to offset changes in airline hiring. Moreover, by basing the WO program size on a company-grade inventory just large enough to sustain field-grade requirements, both field-grade and total pilot inventories would fall short of requirements whenever CO retention dipped below the expected level used to size the WO program.[4] Finally, because of lower expected retention, particularly when demand for commercial pilots is high, a WO component would increase pilot production requirements, possibly to a level exceeding feasible production or absorption constraints.

---

[4] Inventory shortfalls are a risk in any context in which inventory gains (e.g., accessions, promotions) predicated on projected retention are sized so as to exactly meet requirements. For the pilot inventory, the risk is magnified by the criticality of the pilot inventory in meeting senior leadership requirements. See discussion under "Aircrew Management Dynamics" in Chapter One.

Chapter Three. An Aviation Technical Track

As an alternative to reintroduction of WOs in the Air Force, we examined a close alternative—implementing an ATT for COs. Because our analysis found the ATT to be a more attractive option for the Air Force than a WO component, we also provide recommendations regarding key policy decisions that must be addressed in implementing an ATT.

In recent Air Force pilot retention deliberations, the broad outlines of an ATT have been proposed. The concept generally includes providing to a limited number of COs a career path that is focused exclusively, or nearly so, on jobs that require continuous flying duties. It would target officers who miss key developmental opportunities or who would choose to forgo such opportunities either to focus on flying or perhaps to obtain a preferred work/life balance. Officers on a technical track would be less prepared for, and therefore less likely to be placed in, leadership positions. They would also tend to fare poorly in traditional officer promotion processes, which tend to reward breadth in leadership competencies over depth in technical competencies.

To provide a retention-enhancing career path for officers in an ATT, the track should provide

- a defined duty set
- greater assignment stability
- predictable, reasonably attractive promotion outcomes
- a clear path to retirement by removing risks of involuntary separation.

The latter two conditions present the greatest challenge for personnel policy management. Because of their more limited professional development, there is general agreement that some level of promotion opportunity should be afforded for those in the ATT but at measuredly lower rates than those of traditional-track officers, and their promotion timing would be later than that of traditional-track officers. To avoid the risk of involuntary separation prior to retirement eligibility, the timing of consideration for promotion to O-5 should be such that a second failure of selection would occur within seven months of reaching 18 years of active service.[1] Promotion outcomes calibrated to meet these objectives can be obtained by placing ATT officers in a separate competitive category for promotion consideration.

---

[1] 10 U.S.C. § 632(a) requires separation of any officer twice failed of selection for promotion no later than seven months after the president approves a promotion list, unless the date of separation would fall within two years of retirement eligibility or unless that officer is selected for continuation per 10 U.S.C. § 637(a).

Force Structure Considerations

To evaluate the impacts of an ATT, we needed to first define its essential characteristics. Although the Army aviation WO program provided an approximate model for a similar Air Force program, no model currently exists for an ATT. Accordingly, to give definition to the concept, this section provides recommendations regarding the broader terms of an ATT.

Flying Versus Nonflying Requirements

The ATT would be intended specifically to exclude assignment to nonflying positions. Accordingly, design of the ATT should consider the career points at which nonflying positions might be encountered. As indicated in Table 3.1, regular (active-component) Air Force nonflying positions are found largely at the field-grade level.[2] Having pilots opt into the ATT as CGOs would have negligible impact on their career paths before promotion to the field-grade level and might lead some officers to prematurely foreclose a path to senior leadership positions. Accordingly, we recommend an ATT that focuses on FGOs.

Table 3.1. Regular Air Force Pilot Requirements, Fiscal Year 2018

Grade	Flying	Nonflying	Total	Percentage Nonflying
Company	8,214	107	8,321	1.3
Field	2,991	1,618	4,609	35.1
Total	11,205	1,725	12,930	

SOURCE: AF/A3TF.
NOTE: Excludes remotely piloted aircraft pilots; includes O-1 to O-5 only; includes pilot allocation of student, transient, and institutional requirements.

Recommended Characteristics

Although we recognize that refinements would emerge as such a proposal moved toward implementation, the recommendations provided here are those we thought would best achieve the objectives of the program. They closely match those of a proposal developed at a dedicated aircrew retention team summit held at Charleston Air Force Base, South Carolina, in August 2017.

Entry into the Aviation Technical Track

We recommend a program that is open to O-4s and O-5s, with entry permitted after selection for promotion to either of those grades but prior to in-the-promotion-zone (IPZ) consideration to

---

[2] As in the WO discussion in Chapter Two, only O-4 and O-5 positions and individuals are included in pilot field-grade counts.

the next-higher grade.[3] For O-4s, this would mean entry eligibility generally between the 11th and 14th CYOSs. For O-5s, entry would be generally between the 15th and 20th CYOSs.

If the ATT becomes attractive enough to draw more interested applicants than its targeted size will accommodate, a selection process will be required. We visualize that a board process would be used but with selection criteria that emphasize technical qualifications rather than the whole-person approach typically used by promotion boards. This, in turn, might require an evaluation process specific to this purpose that focuses on flying skills and potential.

Active-Duty Service Commitment

The dedicated aircrew retention team summit proposal stipulated an ADSC extending from the point of entry into the ATT to 18 YOSs. The rationale was to ensure that every entrant into the ATT would be retained as well as or better than they would have been without an ATT. We viewed this element of the proposal less favorably. For those entering the ATT at the earliest opportunity, the ADSC would be eight years. A lengthy ADSC at that point would likely make the ATT unattractive to some potential entrants, reducing its impact as a retention incentive. Conversely, many of those willing to accept lengthy ADSCs might have already decided to remain in service to retirement; their retention would be unaffected by entry into the ATT. Additionally, ADSCs are intended to provide a return on investment of "money and/or time in training, education, and bonuses" (Secretary of the Air Force, 2012, p. 5). Because entry into the ATT entails no such additional investment, there is no basis for seeking a return.

Promotions

As previously discussed, officers in the ATT would be placed in their own competitive category in order to obtain promotion outcomes consistent with the intent of the program. Promotion opportunities would be lower than those in the traditional line of the Air Force (LAF) competitive category, and phase points would be later. Table 3.2 indicates approximate prevailing opportunities and phase points for the LAF competitive category and those we believe would work well for the ATT competitive category.

---

[3] Applying promotion-zone definitions from 10 U.S.C. § 645, officers who compete IPZ but fail selection in the traditional competitive category would then compete above the promotion zone (APZ) if they were to switch to the ATT competitive category. They would be considered in the ATT competitive category only when they were senior to the senior officer IPZ in the ATT competitive category. We believe that this would create statutorily permissible but unusual promotion consideration circumstances and therefore recommend that it not be permitted as long as other viable candidates are available to fill the ATT to its planned size.

Table 3.2. Current Line of the Air Force and Recommended Aviation Technical-Track Promotion Parameters

Grade	Competitive Category	Opportunity, as a Percentage	IPZ Timing (Pin-On), in CYOSs	IPZ Timing (Board Date), in CYOSs	Below-the-Promotion-Zone Consideration
O-5	Current LAF	~85	~15	14	Yes
	Recommended ATT	~50	~18	17	No
O-6	Current LAF	~50	~21	20	Yes
	Recommended ATT	~25	~24	23	No

Our recommended opportunity rate for ATT O-5 promotions (50 percent) is intended to provide an appropriate incentive for officers to enter the ATT—far enough below the LAF opportunity rate that those in the traditional track would not perceive an unfair advantage for those in the ATT, but high enough to attract appropriately qualified officers to the ATT. In practice, this rate would be adjusted over time to provide the desired incentive for entry into the ATT.

The timing of O-5 ATT boards is set so that an officer twice failed of selection would reach retirement eligibility without being subject to a selective continuation board. That requires the first APZ consideration to be timed so that, when the president approves the report of the board, all twice-deferred officers are within seven months of reaching 18 YOSs (see 10 U.S.C. § 632[a]). That puts the timing of the board at which the first APZ consideration occurs in the middle of the 18th CYOS for the most junior APZ candidate in the ATT; hence the timing for the IPZ board in the middle of the 17th CYOS for the most junior IPZ candidate in the ATT.

The ATT opportunity rate for promotion to O-6 is set with considerations similar to those for the ATT O-5 rate. The timing is set so as to give ATT officers about the same O-5 time in grade as due-course LAF officers promoted to O-6. In practice, our modeling shows that very few ATT O-5s will retain to the 23rd YOS we have recommended for the IPZ board timing, so flexibility in these parameters will be possible with minimal impact on LAF O-6 selections. The ATT O-6 selection rate and timing could be calibrated so as to provide desired retention effects for O-5s with more than 20 YOSs.

Off-Ramps

Some officers opting for the ATT might have second thoughts regarding that decision. Although they might have burned some developmental bridges, we recommend that they be given the latitude to rejoin the traditional track. To avoid promotion-zone definition problems, they should do so before LAF officers with the same time in grade reach their IPZ consideration.[4]

Assignments

Relieved of the move-generating effects of command assignments, professional military education, and staff tours, assignment stability generally exceeding four years on station should not be hard to achieve. We recommend setting four years on station as a minimum, with exceptions for such conditions as mission changes affecting an ATT officer's base of assignment.

The set of job types to which ATT officers can be assigned should be well defined, primarily so that the expectations of officers entering the ATT will be properly formed. Additionally, because the ATT is intended to create assignment patterns that match well to individual preferences, we recommend that policies allow *voluntary* assignment of ATT officers to nonflying jobs. Grounded pilots would presumably continue to be covered by ATT assignment stability policies and would continue to be considered for promotion in the ATT competitive category but would become available for assignments to meet the needs of the Air Force.

Conceivably, traditional-track pilots selected for a nonflying assignment could be allowed a seven-day option to enter the ATT rather than separate in lieu of the assignment. However, this might be infeasible if a selection board is required to regulate entry into the ATT.

Manpower Requirements

We recommend against identifying specific pilot manpower authorizations as ATT billets. Instead, both ATT and traditional-track officers would be assigned against a common subset of flying requirements. Keeping the ATT/traditional-track mix in various organizations within acceptable ranges would be managed through aggregate objectives. For example, policies might stipulate the maximum proportion of ATT officers in various units, locations, or job types. This approach would provide more flexibility in assignments than the alternative of designating specific positions for ATT incumbents and would make it easier to achieve stability objectives for ATT officers.

Aviation Technical-Track Grade Ceilings

As a separate competitive category, the ATT would remain under the officer grade ceilings established at 10 U.S.C. § 523(a)(1). In addition to the LAF category, the other categories sharing the grade ceiling are chaplain, judge advocate general, nurse, medical service, and biomedical service. Only medical officer and dentist categories are exempt from the ceilings.

---

[4] Per 10 U.S.C. § 645, IPZ eligibles are those who have not failed of selection to the next-higher grade and are senior to the junior eligible officer IPZ defined by the service secretary. APZ eligibles are those who are senior to the senior eligible officer IPZ. An ATT officer rejoining the LAF competitive category after its IPZ consideration would fit both the IPZ and APZ definitions, resulting in promotion-zone ambiguity.

Although service secretaries have latitude in how they distribute grade ceilings to each of the competitive categories, 10 U.S.C. § 622 requires that they consider the following:

> (1) the number of positions needed to accomplish mission objectives which require officers of such competitive category in the grade to which the board will recommend officers for promotion, (2) the estimated number of officers needed to fill vacancies in such positions during the period in which it is anticipated that officers selected for promotion will be promoted, and (3) the number of officers authorized by the Secretary of the military department concerned to serve on active duty in the grade and competitive category under consideration.

As a practical matter, the grade ceilings are distributed to current competitive categories more or less in proportion to each category's share of funded manpower authorizations in the grade. This is fundamentally a *requirement-based* approach. It results in differences in promotion opportunity and timing among the competitive categories, such that categories with field-grade requirements richer than their company-grade requirements or lower retention rates tend to have better promotion opportunity or earlier phase points. If differences become too extreme, a service secretary can adjust the grade distribution to make promotion timing and opportunity more consistent across the competitive categories—an *outcome-based* approach.

If our recommendation against earmarking specific positions as ATT requirements were followed, a requirement-based approach for allocating grade ceilings to the ATT competitive category would not be possible. Moreover, an outcome-based approach could be more precisely calibrated to enable the program to meet its objectives. The promotion timing and opportunity for officers in the ATT would be set so as to provide an appropriate incentive for entry into the ATT without creating unfair advantages relative to the LAF competitive category.

Sizing the Aviation Technical Track

As indicated in our discussion of retention impacts, the ATT must be sized so that its adverse impacts on traditional-track officers are minimized. The two concerns are possible adverse promotion opportunity and timing impacts and a greater proportion of traditional-track careers spent in nonflying jobs.

Promotion outcomes for the LAF category might be adversely affected, depending on how much grade ceiling would be required in the ATT to achieve the desired promotion outcomes in that category. The impact on the LAF, whether positive or negative, would be small because the LAF category would be much larger than the ATT category. Determining the specific impacts will require exercising the Air Force's promotion planning model. Preparing and exercising that model is beyond the scope of the research underlying this report but should be done as part of an ATT implementation plan.

Distribution of nonflying jobs is a more critical issue in sizing the ATT. As indicated in Table 3.3, we estimate that about 28 percent of field-grade pilots are currently in nonflying positions. This percentage, however, is based on a current pilot force that is unusually rich in field-grade inventory because of past pilot training production and retention patterns. As also indicated in Table 3.3, if expected retention levels hold over a long period and if production and absorption capacities are sufficient to maintain the required total inventory, the field-grade inventory will decline and the proportion filling nonflying positions will rise to about 32 percent.[5] Because ATT officers will generally not fill nonflying jobs, the ATT can be sized so that the proportion of officers in the traditional track filling nonflying positions stays within a specified limit. Table 3.4 shows these calculations for limits of 35, 40, 45, and 50 percent, assuming the steady-state field-grade inventory (5,032) indicated in Table 3.3. Of these options, the 40-percent level seems tolerable from the perspective of officers in the traditional track while yielding an ATT large enough to justify the administrative burden of managing it. Using these considerations, the recommended ATT size rounds to about 1,000 field-grade pilots.

Table 3.3. Types of Positions Filled by Current and Steady-State Field-Grade Pilot Inventories

FGOs	Current	Steady State
In flying FGO positions	2,991	2,991
In nonflying FGO positions	1,618	1,618
In CGO positions	1,249	423
Total FGOs	5,858	5,032
Percentage in nonflying positions	27.6%	32.2%

SOURCE: Current inventory and position requirements: AF/A3TF.

Table 3.4. Aviation Technical-Track Size as a Function of Limits on Nonflying Assignments for Traditional-Track Field-Grade Officers

FGOs	Percentage of Traditional-Track FGOs in Nonflying Positions			
	35	40	45	50
Traditional track in flying positions	3,005	2,427	1,978	1,618
Traditional track in nonflying positions	1,618	1,618	1,618	1,618
Total traditional track	4,623	4,045	3,596	3,236
ATT	409	987	1,437	1,796
Total	5,032	5,032	5,032	5,032

SOURCE: Position requirements: AF/A3TF.
NOTE: Because of rounding, some totals do not sum precisely.

---

[5] Our estimate of the steady-state field-grade pilot inventory is based on the higher retention continuation rates used to construct Figure 2.1 in Chapter Two but scaled to the size of the total pilot requirement rather than to the field-grade requirement. Those continuation rates yield 12.99 years of TARS, which breaks down into 7.94 company-grade or 5.06 field-grade years. Dividing the total pilot requirement (12,930) by total TARS (12.99) yields the annual pilot training production requirement (995). Multiplying the production requirement by the company-grade and field-grade TARS, respectively, yields the expected steady-state inventories (7,898 CGOs and 5,032 FGOs).

Expected Inventories

Using the higher retention rates depicted in Figure 2.1 in Chapter Two, we developed an inventory projection model to visualize how the ATT might be formed. We found that the target size of 1,000 pilots in the ATT could be achieved by allowing entry of 17 percent of each O-4 year group and 7 percent of each O-5 year group in the CYOS windows discussed above (tenth to 15th YOS for O-4s and 15th to 21st YOS for O-5s). Other combinations of O-4 and O-5 entry rates would also work.

The first model year specifies the beginning inventory with no officers in the ATT (we used the end–FY 2017 inventory count from AF/A3TF). For the second model year, we allowed entries at the 17- and 7-percent rates from all year groups in the specified entry windows. In subsequent model years, we allowed entries at these rates only from the year–group cohorts that had just aged into the entry windows.[6] Assuming a favorable retention impact for those in the ATT, we boosted continuation rates by 3 percent for those in the ATT.[7] Also, assuming some negative retention impact on the non-ATT pilot force, we reduced their continuation rates by 0.3 percent after the tenth YOS. The results are shown in Figure 3.1.

---

[6] In practice, entries might be allowed each year from every eligible year group. To maintain a steady flow through the ATT, we recommend establishing quotas for the size of the ATT in each year group. After the first year in the window, entries would be allowed only to replace losses up to the established quota.

[7] We did not add 3 percentage points to each year's continuation rate. Rather, we multiplied each rate by 1.03. The effect is cumulative, such that, by the tenth year of the model projection, the ATT has grown to about 1,000 pilots; without a continuation rate adjustment, the inventory would be about 900 pilots at that point.

Figure 3.1. Expected Traditional-Track and Aviation Technical-Track Inventories

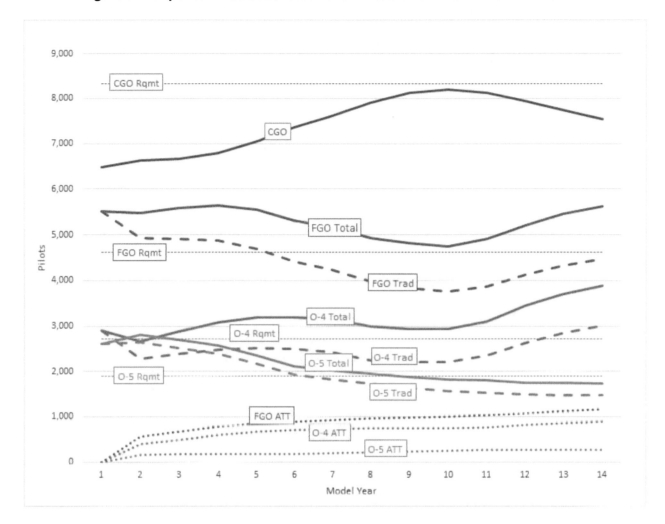

NOTE: Rqmt = requirement. Trad = traditional track.

Promotions from O-4 to O-5 occur in the model at an 85-percent rate in the 15th YOS in the traditional track and at a 50-percent rate in the 18th YOS for those in the ATT. Promotions from O-5 to O-6 are not explicitly modeled because they are implicit in the continuation rates.[8] We note, however, that the remaining ATT inventory at the point at which we recommend consideration for promotion to O-6 (the 23rd YOS) is so small that such promotions would be rare.

Pilot production figures used in the model are 793 and 970 for model years 2 and 3, corresponding to the expected production in FYs 2018 and 2019. Starting in model year 3, we raised this to 1,100 (a current aircrew management objective) but reduced it to 1,000 in model

---

[8] Because the aircrew inventory counts favored by AF/A3TF and other aircrew managers exclude O-6s, the continuation rates developed for aircrew inventory modeling consider separations, retirements, and promotions to O-6 as losses from the inventory.

year 7 and further reduced it to 900 in model year 9 to keep total strength near the current requirement level (approximately 13,000 pilots).

The model depicts the inventories in the ATT stabilizing at the target size of 1,000 after about model year 7 but rising slightly above that figure in the last few years of the projection. In practice, the size would be regulated by varying annual ATT entry rates. The model demonstrates, however, that relatively stable entry rates would produce a relatively stable ATT inventory.

Other interesting trends are evident in the projections from this model. A drop in the field-grade inventory is expected as larger past training production cohorts age out of the force and are replaced by smaller, more recent cohorts. However, even with this drop, the field-grade inventory would remain above requirements. The ATT field-grade inventory would be about 80-percent O-4 and 20-percent O-5; compare these with ranges of 50- to 60-percent O-4 and 40- to 50-percent O-5 in the traditional track.

Retention

It is reasonable to expect that retention would improve for officers opting to enter an ATT, but for different reasons depending on their promotion outlooks. Pilots on weak career paths (e.g., no resident professional military education, no jobs above unit level, no officer performance report pushes or stratification, a "promote" recommendation on a previous promotion recommendation form) might see their promotion expectations elevated in the ATT. Elevated promotion expectations would arguably increase their retention propensities. Pilots on strong career paths but who prefer not to pursue promotion-enhancing education or experience might see reduced promotion expectations in the ATT but would opt for the ATT because they see some greater offsetting utility in its other features. Overall greater satisfaction with the ATT career path would tend to enhance pilots' retention propensities.

Data from a crowdsourcing pulse survey of Air Force aircrew members conducted by the Air Force's Aircrew Crisis Task Force in December 2017 through January 2018 (Department of the Air Force, 2018) tend to support these retention expectations. The survey pulsed a sample of about 7,900 officer and enlisted aircrew members in all grades, with a response rate of about 33 percent. In response to an item worded "Opportunity for a 'technical fly-only track' would influence me to stay in the [Air Force] longer," 2,438 respondents provided ratings that were 73-percent positive, 13-percent neutral, and 14-percent negative.

However, in setting the terms for an ATT, its impacts on retention of officers remaining in the traditional career track must also be considered. At least two such considerations apply. First, with pilots in the ATT no longer filling a share of nonflying pilot requirements, pilots in the traditional track would spend greater proportions of their careers in those positions. For at least some traditional-track pilots, this would likely reduce retention propensities. Additionally, there is a possibility that promotion outcomes for pilots in the traditional track would be slightly diminished by the increased retention and grade tenures of pilots in the ATT. In an examination of officer management flexibilities that included a much larger set of technical tracks than the one contemplated for the pilot workforce, Robbert, Terry, et al. (2017) reports such an effect. This too would tend to reduce retention propensities for officers in the traditional track. Minimizing these impacts would be a key consideration in determining the number of officers to be admitted to an ATT.

Costs

Given the increased retention expected with an ATT, force costs would rise somewhat. With no change in total officer strength, there would be no change in officer grade strengths. However, the YOS distribution in grades O-4 and O-5 would be expected to increase slightly as a result of longer tenures of ATT officers in those grades, slightly increasing the average rate of pay in those grades. With better retention and no change in force size, training costs would decrease.[9]

We estimated the changes in cost for a workforce with 1,000 officers in the ATT, compared with their costs without an ATT, assuming that continuation rates would increase by 3 percent in the 11th through 20th YOSs for those in the ATT. Our base case for this cost analysis used the higher retention rates depicted in Figure 2.1 in Chapter Two. Training production requirements are 184.2 and 175.6 for the two cases, or a reduction of 8.6 pilot training production requirements per year in the ATT case to maintain a total workforce of 2,394 pilots, including those in the first ten YOSs prior to entering the ATT.[10] The base pay increases due to a shift in distribution across pay steps for 1,000 FGOs were $499,000 per year, expanded to $641,000 to include the NCP (28.4 percent) for the Air Force's payment into the DoD retirement accrual fund.[11] Training costs would be reduced by the variable costs indicated in Table 2.4 in Chapter Two, ranging from $1 million to $6.7 million per graduate. An annual reduction of 8.6 pilot training graduates would yield savings of many multiples of the personnel cost increases.

We also assumed that retention of officers in the traditional track would decrease by 0.3 percent. We calculated an additional 4.1 production requirements as a result of this decrease, consuming about half of the savings associated with improved retention of ATT officers.

---

[9] An obvious exception would be years in which production capacity would be insufficient to meet requirements. In those cases, personnel costs would go up but pilot production, and hence training costs, would not be reduced.

[10] The total pilot inventory maintained with these production levels is greater than 1,000 because pilots in the first ten YOSs are not in the ATT.

[11] We did not include other elements of RMC in this analysis because they are grade-dependent rather than YOS-dependent and would thus be the same for both the base case and the ATT case. Total officer strength, and thus total field-grade strength, are the same in both the base and ATT cases.

Risks

As noted in discussions above, several uncertainties could affect the retention of officers in the traditional track. First, the impact of an increased proportion of nonflying assignments in the careers of traditional-track officers is unknown. Second, promotion outcomes for officers in the traditional track could be adversely affected (although the size of the effect, if any, is expected to be small). A third consideration is that reduced availability of flying jobs for traditional-track officers could cause a greater number to miss their third AvIP gates, reducing their military earnings and thus their retention.[12] Finally, particularly for fighter pilots, there is a concern that traditional-track pilots might see too little time in *operational* fighter squadrons prior to assignment as squadron commanders. Except for the proportion of nonflying assignments, we believe that these risks are minimal, but they merit further investigation prior to implementation of an ATT.

---

[12] Per 37 U.S.C. § 301a(a)(4), to be continuously entitled to monthly AvIP through 25 years of aviation service, an officer must perform operational flying duties during at least 12 of the first 18 years of aviation service. This is the third of three "gates" used to determine the duration of entitlements to continuous monthly AvIP. Aviation service includes flight training, so pilots perform at least nine years of operational flying duties during their ten company-grade years (assuming that pilot training is started no more than one year after commissioning), requiring three more years in operational flying duties as an FGO to meet the third gate. Pilots would complete 18 years of aviation service after 19 CYOSs (again, assuming a one-year wait to enter pilot training). Thus, such a pilot would need to perform operational flying duties during three of the first nine years (33 percent) as an FGO in order to meet the third gate. Our recommended ATT size leaves 60 percent of field-grade time in flying positions, but individual experience would vary around this average. Some officers at the very low end of this distribution might not make their third gates.

Chapter Four. Conclusions

As indicated in Chapter One, we found that force structure considerations would permit either a WO component or an ATT as a supplement to the traditional pilot career path. We arrived through dissimilar considerations at estimates that either alternative could be sized manageably at about 1,000 pilots out of a total requirement of just less than 13,000. A WO component would displace pilots primarily at the company-grade level, while an ATT would be focused on pilot utilization at the field-grade level. Most importantly, with respect to the primary objective of these supplemental paths, the WO alternative would be expected to *reduce* pilot retention, while the ATT would be expected to *increase* it. We compared the costs of either option with those of the current force, finding that cost considerations, although minor, slightly favor the WO option. Both alternatives introduce certain risks, meriting further examination prior to implementing either alternative.

Force Structure Considerations

A WO component in the Air Force pilot force would be limited by the Air Force's need to sustain a pilot inventory that meets field-grade requirements. Using current retention expectations, we estimate that WOs could displace about 1,000 COs if they fill only company-grade positions and about 700 more if they also fill some field-grade positions. If retention declined to lower but plausible levels, the headroom for WOs would total only about 700 if they could fill some field-grade requirements and about 40 if they could fill only company-grade requirements.

We found that an ATT would be useful only in the field-grade segment of the pilot force and would be limited by the need to avoid too high a concentration of nonflying assignments for FGOs in the traditional track. If traditional-track officers are limited to 40 percent of their field-grade tenures in nonflying assignments, an ATT could be sized at about 1,000 officers.

Retention

Neither a WO program nor an ATT has been observed in the retention context of the Air Force pilot workforce—highly trained, at great expense, with very inviting civilian employment opportunities. Lacking explicit empirical data, we estimated retention impacts using econometric modeling, in the case of WOs, and less quantitative comparative utilities, in the case of the ATT. Although we found some exceptions among the aviation communities and levels of MAH demand that we examined, we expect that a WO component would generally have lower retention rates than the CO population it would displace because WOs would, in most cases, see greater differences between their prospective military and civilian earnings. We expect that an

ATT would increase retention for those who choose to enter it because doing so provides career path assurances not otherwise available to them. However, because the ATT could have negative retention impacts on pilots remaining in a traditional track, overall retention considerations become the limiting factor on the size of an ATT.

Costs

Overall costs of a workforce have two major components—*personnel* costs incurred for compensation and benefits and *training* costs to maintain a workforce of the required size. Because pilot training costs are so high, it is possible that factors affecting personnel costs can be either overwhelmed or significantly offset by their impacts on training costs. We found this to be the case for both WO and ATT alternatives but in opposite directions.

A WO component would incur lower personnel costs than the CO workforce it displaced, but the lower compensation levels responsible for the lower personnel costs would also produce lower retention rates. With lower retention, training costs would go up. At the retention levels we anticipate, personnel cost savings would slightly exceed training cost increases, yielding potential net savings of $4 million to $30 million (roughly 1 percent of total pilot personnel and training costs), depending on the retention environment and on the distribution of WOs across various aircrew communities.

The ATT would affect personnel and training costs in directions opposite to those of a WO component. Higher retention would shift the YOS distribution of the force to higher steps in the basic pay table, increasing personnel costs. But personnel cost increases would be relatively modest because grade strengths would not be changed by the ATT. Modest personnel costs would be more than offset by the reduced training costs attributable to improved retention.

For both the WO and ATT alternatives, cost considerations are complicated by inflexibilities in managing pilot production and absorption. If production and absorption capacity cannot be readily expanded, introduction of a WO component would not increase training costs. Rather, it would increase pilot shortages. If existing production and absorption capacity is less than needed to maintain the required pilot force inventory, introduction of an ATT would not reduce training costs, but it would reduce pilot shortages.

Risks

If the Air Force constituted a WO pilot component maximized to the company-grade headroom associated with expected retention, it would risk shortfalls in both total pilot requirements and field-grade requirements if lower retention prevailed. As with COs, the AvB program for WOs would have to be carefully managed to adapt quickly to changes in the civilian demand for pilots and civilian pilot compensation. This is especially true because WOs will, in general, be more sensitive than COs to changes in the civilian labor market because of the greater difference between the expected opportunity wage for WOs when MAH is high than when it is low. Lower retention would also strain the Air Force's training pipeline production and operational unit absorption capacities.

Risks associated with the ATT are related to its impacts on those remaining in the traditional track. These include an increased proportion of nonflying assignments as FGOs, possibly diminished promotion outcomes due to the lengthened tenures of officers in the ATT, reduced availability of flying jobs needed to reach third AvIP gates, and, particularly for fighter pilots, possibly too little time in *operational* squadrons prior to assignment as squadron commanders.

Limitations of time and resources prevented us from fully examining these risks in the analyses conducted for this report. They merit further research before either alternative is implemented.

Comparisons

Table 4.1 summarizes the findings of this quick-response study. Because the fundamental objective of either supplemental path is to enhance retention, particularly when the demand for commercial pilots is high, the ATT is clearly favored. Both would yield modest cost savings, and both would present risks yet to be fully evaluated. Not least, a WO program would require development and management of new processes and policies across the personnel life cycle— recruiting, accessions, compensation, retention, utilization, promotion, and transition. An ATT would require much less sweeping adjustments, most of which would be managed through the creation of a new competitive category.

Table 4.1. Comparison of Key Factors

Factor	WO Component	ATT
Retention	−	+
Production and absorption requirements	+	−
Personnel costs	−	+
Training costs	+	−
Net costs	−	−
Administrative requirements	+ Need to manage the life cycle of a new personnel category	− Need to establish a new competitive category
Risks	Retention is more sensitive to MAH; possible field-grade and total pilot shortages if retention is less than planned	Possible retention impacts on traditional-track officers (more nonflying assignments, adverse promotion outcomes, missing third AvIP gates, less operational experience)

References

Bigelow, James H., and Albert A. Robbert, *Balancing Rated Personnel Requirements and Inventories*, Santa Monica, Calif.: RAND Corporation, TR-869-AF, 2011. As of February 24, 2018:
https://www.rand.org/pubs/technical_reports/TR869.html

Bigelow, James H., Bill Taylor, Craig Moore, and Brent Thomas, *Models of Operational Training in Fighter Squadrons*, Santa Monica, Calif.: RAND Corporation, MR-1701-AF, 2003. As of February 27, 2018:
https://www.rand.org/pubs/monograph_reports/MR1701.html

Department of the Air Force, Aircrew Crisis Task Force, *U.S. Air Force Optimize Aircrew Retention Crowdsourcing Pulse 1*, briefing, February 9, 2018, not available to the general public.

DoD—*See* U.S. Department of Defense.

Fernandez, Richard L., *The Warrant Officer Ranks: Adding Flexibility to Military Personnel Management*, Washington, D.C.: Congressional Budget Office, February 2002. As of June 7, 2018:
https://www.cbo.gov/publication/13513

Jones, Darrell, *Warrant Officers*, unpublished Air Force briefing, July 22, 2008, not available to the general public.

Mattock, Michael G., James Hosek, Beth J. Asch, and Rita Karam, *Retaining U.S. Air Force Pilots When the Civilian Demand for Pilots Is Growing*, Santa Monica, Calif.: RAND Corporation, RR-1455-AF, 2016. As of March 5, 2018:
https://www.rand.org/pubs/research_reports/RR1455.html

Mosher, Frederick C., *Democracy and the Public Service*, New York: Oxford University Press, 1982.

Office of the Under Secretary of Defense for Personnel and Readiness, Directorate of Compensation, *Selected Military Compensation Tables*, January 1, 2018. As of May 21, 2018:
http://militarypay.defense.gov/Portals/3/Documents/Reports/GreenBook%202018.pdf?ver=2018-01-16-123652-020

Robbert, Albert A., Anthony D. Rosello, C. R. Anderegg, John A. Ausink, James H. Bigelow, Bill Taylor, and James Pita, *Reducing Air Force Fighter Pilot Shortages*, Santa Monica, Calif.: RAND Corporation, RR-1113-AF, 2015. As of February 24, 2018: https://www.rand.org/pubs/research_reports/RR1113.html

Robbert, Albert A., Tara L. Terry, Alexander D. Rothenberg, Anthony Lawrence, and Neil Brian Carey, *Air Force Officer Management Flexibilities: Modeling Potential Policies*, Santa Monica, Calif.: RAND Corporation, RR-1921-AF, 2017. As of April 16, 2018: https://www.rand.org/pubs/research_reports/RR1921.html

Secretary of the Air Force, *Personnel: Active Duty Service Commitments (ADSC)*, Air Force Instruction 36-2107, April 30, 2012. As of May 11, 2018: http://static.e-publishing.af.mil/production/1/af_a1/publication/afi36-2107/afi36-2107.pdf

Taylor, Bill, James H. Bigelow, and John A. Ausink, *Fighter Drawdown Dynamics: Effects on Aircrew Inventories*, Santa Monica, Calif.: RAND Corporation, MG-855-AF, 2009. As of February 24, 2018: https://www.rand.org/pubs/monographs/MG855.html

Taylor, Bill, James H. Bigelow, Craig Moore, Leslie Wickman, Brent Thomas, and Richard S. Marken, *Absorbing Air Force Fighter Pilots: Parameters, Problems, and Policy Options*, Santa Monica, Calif.: RAND Corporation, MR-1550-AF, 2002. As of February 24, 2018: https://www.rand.org/pubs/monograph_reports/MR1550.html

Taylor, Bill, Craig Moore, and Charles Robert Roll, Jr., *The Air Force Pilot Shortage: A Crisis for Operational Units?* Santa Monica, Calif.: RAND Corporation, MR-1204-AF, 2000. As of February 24, 2018: https://www.rand.org/pubs/monograph_reports/MR1204.html

U.S. Code, Title 10, Armed Forces; Subtitle A, General Military Law; Part II, Personnel; Chapter 32, Officer Strength and Distribution in Grade; Section 523, Authorized Strengths: Commissioned Officers on Active Duty in Grades of Major, Lieutenant Colonel, and Colonel and Navy Grades of Lieutenant Commander, Commander, and Captain. As of June 9, 2018: https://www.gpo.gov/fdsys/granule/USCODE-2010-title10/ USCODE-2010-title10-subtitleA-partII-chap32-sec523/content-detail.html

U.S. Code, Title 10, Armed Forces; Subtitle A, General Military Law; Part II, Personnel; Chapter 36, Promotion, Separation and Involuntary Retirement of Officers on the Active-Duty List; Subchapter II, Promotions; Section 622, Numbers to Be Recommended for Promotion. As of June 9, 2018: https://www.gpo.gov/fdsys/granule/USCODE-1996-title10/ USCODE-1996-title10-subtitleA-partII-chap36-subchapII-sec622

U.S. Code, Title 10, Armed Forces; Subtitle A, General Military Law; Part II, Personnel; Chapter 36, Promotion, Separation, and Involuntary Retirement of Officers on the Active-Duty List; Subchapter III, Failure of Selection for Promotion and Retirement for Years of Service; Section 632, Effect of Failure of Selection for Promotion: Captains and Majors of the Army, Air Force, and Marine Corps and Lieutenants and Lieutenant Commanders of the Navy. As of June 9, 2018:
https://www.gpo.gov/fdsys/granule/USCODE-2010-title10/
USCODE-2010-title10-subtitleA-partII-chap36-subchapIII-sec632

U.S. Code, Title 10, Armed Forces; Subtitle A, General Military Law; Part II, Personnel; Chapter 36, Promotion, Separation, and Involuntary Retirement of Officers on the Active-Duty List; Subchapter IV, Continuation on Active Duty and Selective Early Retirement; Section 637, Selection of Regular Officers for Continuation on Active Duty. As of June 9, 2018:
https://www.gpo.gov/fdsys/granule/USCODE-2010-title10/
USCODE-2010-title10-subtitleA-partII-chap36-subchapIV-sec637

U.S. Code, Title 10, Armed Forces; Subtitle A, General Military Law; Part II, Personnel; Chapter 36, Promotion, Separation, and Involuntary Retirement of Officers on the Active-Duty List; Subchapter V, Additional Provisions Relating to Promotion, Separation, and Retirement; Section 645, Definitions. As of June 9, 2018:
https://www.gpo.gov/fdsys/granule/USCODE-2010-title10/
USCODE-2010-title10-subtitleA-partII-chap36-subchapV-sec645

U.S. Code, Title 37, Pay and Allowances of the Uniformed Services; Chapter 5, Special and Incentive Pays; Section 301a, Incentive Pay: Aviation Career. As of June 11, 2018:
https://www.gpo.gov/fdsys/granule/USCODE-1994-title37/
USCODE-1994-title37-chap5-sec301a

U.S. Department of Defense, *Fiscal Year 2017: Military Retirement Fund Audited Financial Report*, November 6, 2017. As of May 21, 2018:
https://www.oversight.gov/sites/default/files/oig-reports/DODIG-2018-012.pdf